Operation Noble Eagle

The War on Terrorism

By John Hamilton

Visit us at
www.abdopub.com

Printed in the United States.

Edited by Paul Joseph
Graphic Design: John Hamilton
Cover Design: Mighty Media
Photos: AP/Wide World, Corbis, DoD, PhotoSpin

Library of Congress Cataloging-in-Publication Data

Hamilton, John 1959-
    Operation Noble Eagle / John Hamilton.
        p. cm. — (War on terrorism)
    Includes index.
    Summary: Looks at the history of homeland defense in the United States and changes that were made after the terrorist attacks of September 11, 2001, especially the development of the Office of Homeland Security.
    ISBN 1-57765-664-4
    1. War on terrorism, 2001—Juvenile literature. 2. Terrorism—United States—Prevention—Juvenile literature. 3. National Security—United States—Juvenile literature. 4. Emergency management—United States—Juvenile literature. 5. United States—Defenses—Juvenile literature. [1. War on terrorism, 2001- 2. United States—Office of Homeland Security. 3. Terrorism. 4. National security. 5. Emergency management. 6. United States—Politics and government—2001-.] I. Title. II. Series.

HV6432.H35 2002
973.931—dc21

2001056656

Table of Contents

America Under Siege

The twin towers of the World Trade Center burn after the September 11 attack. The Empire State Building stands in the foreground.

Homeland Defense

N SEPTEMBER 11, 2001, MOST AMERICANS became aware that terrorism isn't something that only happens on foreign soil, in out-of-the-way corners of the Middle East, or other far-off destinations. Now Americans know just how vulnerable they are. Terrorism can cross the oceans and strike at the very heart of America.

After the devastation of the September 11 attacks on New York City and Washington, D.C., President George W. Bush commanded the armed forces to do more to protect security at home, as well as carry out their traditional role in conflicts overseas. Operation Noble Eagle was the name given to the military effort to protect the homeland of the United States from terrorism.

This wasn't the first time the U.S. homeland came under siege in wartime. During the War of 1812, British soldiers looted and burned most of Washington, D.C. In 1942, during World War II, eight German spies were carried by submarine to the East Coast of the United States. The Germans had orders to spread terror by blowing up key industrial sites, including hydroelectric plants, railroads, and businesses. Fortunately, the spies were quickly captured, and no damage was done.

In addition to enlisting the help of the armed forces, President Bush also expanded the role of the Federal Bureau of Investigation (FBI) in fighting terrorism. Before September 11, the FBI's main focus was on crime solving. For now, that role has shifted to crime prevention, with the arrest and interrogation of thousands of people who might have information about possible terrorist cells, or groups, operating in the United States.

The Anti-Terrorism Act of 2001 is a set of laws that gives the FBI broad new powers in its fight against terrorism. The laws give federal crime fighters more leeway in tapping suspects' phones and computers. The laws also allow for immigrants suspected of terrorism to be held for up to seven days without being charged with a crime. This gives the FBI more time to question suspected terrorists and to build a better case against them in court. (Before the new laws, immigrants had to be released within 48 hours unless charged with a specific crime.)

Finding out who the terrorists are before they strike is one goal in the war on terrorism. Finding out how, when, and where they might attack is an even larger task. The United States prides itself on being a free and open society. Unfortunately, that very freedom makes it easier for terrorists to slip in unnoticed and carry out their missions of destruction.

The dangers are many. In addition to turning America's own technology against itself (such as piloting jets into buildings), terrorists may have a whole range of weapons at their disposal. These might include conventional, biological, chemical, and even nuclear weapons. Weapons of mass destruction are so horrifying that many people are almost paralyzed with fear. But the terrorists of September 11 didn't need weapons of mass destruction to paralyze the U.S. They did it with a handful of commercial airliners.

Law Enforcement On Alert

FBI agents check the identification of a postal worker. Law enforcement authorities went on heightened alert after the September 11 attacks.

Combat Air Patrol

F-16A Fighting Falcons from the North Dakota Air National Guard patrol the skies over Washington, D.C. The damaged Pentagon can be seen between the two jets.

Happy Hooligans

ND
AF
82 006

Happy Hooligans

ND
AF
82 992

Many people in the Defense Department don't think future terrorists will bother with weapons of mass destruction—they're too hard to get and too hard to use. Instead, they'll probably use conventional weapons such as guns and bombs to strike the U.S. at its weak spots. Said one official at the Pentagon, "There are hundreds of these targets, and attacking them with conventional means—a truck full of explosives—is a heck of a lot easier than building an atom bomb or a chemical weapon."

Operation Noble Eagle aims to meet each of these challenges head-on. It won't be easy, but with the future of the United States at stake, the men and women in the armed forces and law enforcement are eager to rise to the challenge.

Tom Ridge

Director of Homeland Security Tom Ridge briefs reporters at the White House on terrorism threats within the United States.

Office Of Homeland Security

**S**HORTLY AFTER THE TERRORIST ATTACKS OF September 11, President Bush created the Office of Homeland Security. Its director is former Pennsylvania Governor Tom Ridge, who is now responsible for helping the United States prepare for future terrorist attacks. Director Ridge is an honored combat veteran and a strong national leader with ties to the White House. He reports directly to President Bush, giving advice and recommending ways to protect the United States from terrorism.

Once the Office of Homeland Security is fully up and running, it will be a central command center for emergency response. If another big terror attack happens, the office will work closely with the already-established Federal Emergency Management Agency (FEMA) to rush supplies and emergency workers to the scene.

Mock terrorist attacks are conducted regularly to prepare people for actual emergencies. Last year, three exercises took place: a mock biological attack in Colorado, a chemical attack in New Hampshire, and a nuclear strike in Washington, D.C. The lessons learned from these and future exercises will help officials prepare for a real attack.

Homeland Security will also try to reinforce defenses at targets that might tempt terrorists. These include places such as power plants, bridges, airports, and sports stadiums. Even amusement parks, such as Disneyland, are tightening security to make sure they are as safe as possible from terrorist attacks.

In the long run, the most important job of the Office of Homeland Security will be to work closely with the National Security Council to plan and coordinate the counter-terrorism work of more than 40 federal agencies. Local and state agencies will also need to learn to work together to fight terrorism.

There are many law-enforcement organizations in the United States. These include local police, state police, the National Guard, the FBI, the Bureau of Alcohol, Tobacco and Firearms (ATF), and the Central Intelligence Agency (CIA). Each of these organizations has its own way of doing things, and its own jurisdiction, or turf. Each also jealously guards information learned in its criminal investigations. Valuable time is often wasted as different agencies argue over who has jurisdiction to investigate certain crimes.

Sometimes agencies overlap in their investigations. For example, an FBI agent may spend days or weeks tracking down leads in a crime, not knowing that the information has already been obtained by the CIA, or vice versa.

On Guard

A soldier with the California National Guard stands watch by the toll plaza of the Golden Gate Bridge in San Francisco, California.

Getting these different agencies to share their information, their "intelligence," is a big priority of the Office of Homeland Security. By working together as a team, America's law enforcement agencies have a much better chance of stopping terrorism in its tracks.

In a January 2002 interview, Director Ridge said that the U.S. is safer now than it was when the World Trade Center and Pentagon were attacked. "Every single day since September 11," he said, "we've made ourselves safer, stronger, and more secure. We still have a lot of work left to do. We're making progress every day."

Planning Strategy

President Bush talks with Tom Ridge, head of the Office of Homeland Security, in the Oval Office at the White House.

Training Exercise

Emergency workers conduct a bio emergency drill in New York City.

Airport Security

A California National Guard soldier, armed with an M-16 rifle, stands guard at the X-ray security screening area at Los Angeles International Airport.

The National Guard

**O**NE OF THE FIRST ACTIONS TAKEN BY Operation Noble Eagle was to activate Air National Guard and Air Force Reserve units to patrol U.S. airspace. Not wanting to be caught off-guard as they were on September 11, the armed forces made themselves ready to intercept and shoot down any airliner that terrorists might hijack and use as a flying bomb. By mid-January, 2002, more than 13,000 fighter-jet patrols had flown round-the-clock, at a cost to taxpayers of more than $324 million. Most of these missions were over New York and Washington, D.C., but other cities also received some air cover. It was the first time since the Cuban Missile Crisis in 1962 that constant combat air patrols protected the skies over the United States.

The U.S. military activates large numbers of reserve troops when it gets ready for war. The Army and Air National Guard are reserve units of the U.S. Army and Air Force. The total number of Reserve and National Guard troops on active duty as of January 23, 2002, was 71,386.

Mobilizing the National Guard is just one way that Operation Noble Eagle aims to protect U.S. shores against terrorism. But putting U.S. National Guard troops on alert has a strong symbolic value. Shortly after the September 11 attacks, President Bush told advisers, "You understand what I am facing. I have to alert the American people to the ongoing dangers without creating alarm and irrational fear." The president decided that one of the quickest and most effective things he could do was send National Guard troops to help with security at airports, bus stations, bridges, the U.S. borders with Canada and Mexico, and to fly combat air patrols over large cities.

Said Craig Duehring at the U.S. Defense Department, "No other single action more clearly demonstrates the national resolve than to mobilize the National Guard and Reserve forces of America."

Guarding A Stricken City

A Vermont Air National Guard F-16 flies over New York City on September 12, 2001.

Stadium Security

A National Guardsman stands at his post outside the Louisiana Superdome in New Orleans, LA, site of Super Bowl XXXVI.

19

Watchful Eyes

A Missouri National Guardsman observes a traveler at the Springfield-Branson Regional Airport, in Springfield, Missouri.

Airline Security

F SPECIAL CONCERN AFTER SEPTEMBER 11 was reinforcing security at the nation's busy commercial airports. About 670 million U.S. airline passengers fly annually. That's a lot of people to check, and the nation's airport security personnel are often underpaid and poorly trained to identify possible terrorists. National Guard troops were sent to major airports to help give extra protection to the flying public.

Before planes even leave the ground, extra security has been put in place. There are tighter restrictions on who can gain access to airline terminals. Ground crew workers, those who work to prepare planes before takeoff, are also subject to tighter background and security checks. Passengers are also more closely scrutinized. In addition to walking through metal detectors, they now must sometimes go through searches of their clothes and carry-on baggage. Long lines at airports are now normal, but passengers seem willing to endure the inconvenience if it means safer skies.

In mid-January 2002, new laws went into effect that required airlines to inspect every piece of luggage that flies on a plane, and to match the luggage to individual passengers. The law is intended to prevent terrorists from placing a bomb in a suitcase without actually getting on the flight. This is how investigators believe terrorists in 1988 destroyed Pan Am Flight 103, which blew up over Lockerbie, Scotland, killing 259 people on board and 11 on the ground.

To inspect the 3.5 million checked bags that fly each day, airlines use several methods, including bomb-sniffing dogs, X-rays, and manual searches. Better training and background checks of airport security workers, especially those operating metal detectors, is also being carried out.

Once jetliners get in the air, several measures have been taken to make flights safer. There are now more federal sky marshals riding aboard airplanes. These are armed, plainclothes police officers who are trained to deal with terrorists. Before September 11, there were about 36 sky marshals covering as many as 30,000 daily flights. Today, that number is much higher, but still not every flight has a sky marshal. However, there are enough on flights today—with more sky marshals being added each week—that terrorists might think twice before hijacking a jetliner. Also, airlines have improved cockpit security, including reinforced and armored doors that separate pilots from the passenger compartments.

One idea for a future security measure is to use biometrics to rapidly identify passengers and perhaps learn beforehand if someone is a known terrorist. Biometrics technology uses computers to identify unique features of the human body, such as fingerprints, the iris of the eye, or even the shape of a face. The technology for these tools already exists. Now it is a matter of putting together a workable system that airports can easily use, and finding a way to pay for it.

Canine Patrol

A police officer and his dog check luggage for bombs at Baltimore-Washington International Airport.

Deadly Package

A vial of germ-laced fluid marked "biohazard," like one that might be stored at a hospital or research facility.

Biological Terror

I N 1984, IN THE TOWN OF THE DALLES, OREGON, THE United States suffered its first known biological weapons attack. Followers of a religious cult led by Bhagwan Shree Rajneesh put salmonella bacteria in drinking glasses and salad bars at several of the town's restaurants. Nobody died, but 750 people were poisoned, suffering nausea, fever, and severe diarrhea.

The Oregon attack proved that criminals and terrorists could use biological weapons. Many experts on terrorism, however, were slow to heed the warning. They insisted that germ weapons are too hard to make and too hard to deliver in order to be effective terrorist tools.

Even after September 11, many scoffed at the notion of a bio attack. One adviser to Congress on the subject of terrorism told *TIME* magazine, "The idea that someone sends a letter through the mail that you open up, and it says, 'Ha-ha, you've just been exposed to anthrax and are going to die'? Not a chance, just not a chance." But of course that is exactly what happened. In October 2001, letters laced with anthrax, a deadly bacteria, showed up in several locations.

25

The anthrax, which appeared as a white powder packed inside the letters, first struck a worker at American Media, in Boca Raton, Florida. Anthrax was soon discovered in the offices of television networks ABC and CBS, the office of New York Governor George Pataki, and the offices of the *New York Post* newspaper. Most alarming of all, anthrax-laced letters addressed to Senators Tom Daschle and Patrick Leahy forced a shutdown of the U.S. House of Representatives as men in white hazardous-materials (hazmat) suits started sweeping for anthrax spores in the Capitol building.

The Hart Senate Office Building, which houses the offices of 50 senators and their staff, was shut down on October 17, 2001, after the letter addressed to Senator Daschle was opened, spreading anthrax spores all over the building. After a lengthy and difficult cleanup by the Environmental Protection Agency (EPA), the office building was finally reopened in January 2002.

In all, five people died after inhaling anthrax spores in Florida, Washington, D.C., New York, and Connecticut. Thirteen other people became ill but recovered after taking antibiotics. Two of those killed were postal workers. They were most likely infected when the tainted letters passed through high-speed mail sorting machines. Experts are still puzzled by how the other three people who died were exposed, but one guess is that their mail somehow came into contact with the tainted letters.

Anthrax is a germ that comes in several forms. It is often found among livestock and wild animals. People can sometimes get anthrax from animals, but these are mostly people who work closely with infected animals, such as slaughterhouse workers.

HART
SENATE OFFICE BUILDING

MEMBERS
AND STAFF
AT ALL TIMES
VISITORS
FROM
9:00A.M.

Hazardous Cleanup

A member of a biohazard team tests for anthrax at the Hart Senate Office Building in Washington, D.C.

CRIME SCENE DO NOT CROSS

To "weaponize" anthrax (to turn it into a bio weapon), the bacteria is dried and turned into spores, which are like microscopic shells. The anthrax bacteria lurk inside the spores, dormant and floating on the breeze, until they are breathed into a human lung. This is called inhalation anthrax, and is the most deadly form of the disease. Anthrax can also be transmitted through the skin, or by ingestion (eating), but these paths are less common and less deadly. Inhalation anthrax, if left untreated, kills 90 percent of those infected.

Once inside a lung, anthrax incubates for two to five days before symptoms appear. When the dormant anthrax bacteria emerge from the spore, they rapidly reproduce and begin producing toxins, which attack the body's vital organs. At first, the victim may show flu-like symptoms, such as fever, nausea,

A Tiny Foe

Anthrax cells are seen in a monkey spleen in this photomicrograph from the U.S. Department of Defense.

The anthrax-laced envelope sent to Senator Tom Daschle.

and coughing. Eventually, high fever and shock sets in, the lungs shut down, and the victim dies. Because at first it mimics the flu, diagnosis of anthrax can be difficult. If it is not identified quickly, it may be too late for the victim.

Fortunately, there are potent drugs available to fight anthrax. If caught in time, even inhalation anthrax can be stopped with antibiotics such as Cipro. There is a vaccine available that has been used by the U.S. Army, but it has troubling side effects. Researchers are now testing for a safe and effective vaccine.

As of January 2002, police are still tracking down the person or group responsible for this latest round of biological terror. At first, Osama bin Laden and his al-Qaeda terrorist network were blamed. But as time has passed, law enforcement officials began quietly searching for a domestic culprit, someone within the United States. Despite a large reward for the criminal's capture, no suspects have yet been caught. But as the war on terrorism continues, it seems that it is only a matter of time before these terrorists are brought to justice.

Smallpox

A child in India is stricken with the smallpox virus in the early 1960s.

Smallpox

Crisis in the Hot Zone is a book about the spread of Ebola, a deadly virus from Africa that dooms most of its victims to a gruesome, painful death. But the virus that scares bio terror experts the most is smallpox, a highly contagious disease that has the potential to infect entire countries in only a few weeks. Smallpox is very deadly, killing about one-third of those infected. As many Native American tribes found out in the 1700s and 1800s, smallpox epidemics race through unprotected populations like wildfire. In the twentieth century alone, smallpox killed an estimated 300 million people.

By the mid-1970s, widespread vaccinations stopped smallpox in its tracks. Officially, the virus was declared wiped out in 1980, although the last known case of smallpox was recorded in 1977. However, two known samples of smallpox remain, one in the U.S. and the other in Russia. It is the Russian sample that has many health experts worried. The Soviet Union once tried to make a bio weapon of smallpox. It is possible that some research samples may have been misplaced, lost, or stolen by terrorists.

If terrorists try to use smallpox as a weapon, they might easily get infected and die themselves. However, as the events of September 11 showed, some terrorists are willing to commit suicide to carry out their missions. Experts fear that one terrorist infected with smallpox could infect thousands of unsuspecting people before dying of the disease.

Most people in the U.S. would be vulnerable to a smallpox epidemic. Routine inoculations against the virus ended in 1972 because a small percentage of people got sick or died. When the worldwide smallpox threat seemed to be over, the vaccinations stopped in order to save the lives of the people who had bad reactions to the vaccine.

People lose most of their protection from the smallpox vaccine in 10 years, but since the virus was officially declared eradicated, protection was no longer needed. Few people thought that smallpox might someday be released on purpose by terrorists. In many ways, the smallpox threat today is a product of modern medicine's success.

To keep the threat of smallpox from turning into a bio-terror nightmare, the U.S. government plans to stockpile 300 million doses of the vaccine by the end of 2002, a big jump from the current supply of 15 million doses.

If there is any bright spot to be optimistic about, it is the fact that weapons made from germs are extremely hard to make. It takes a high level of education, skill, and expensive equipment to turn germs into weapons of terror. Individual terrorists would have a very difficult time making bio weapons and using them to cause mass murder.

State-sponsored terrorists, on the other hand, have the resources of an entire country at their disposal. The focus today is on rogue states like North Korea and Iraq, which support terrorist groups. Iraq, especially, is known to have researched and developed large numbers of biological weapons.

"Black biology" is another area of worry. Genetically altered strains of killer germs could be very difficult to contain. (Imagine a combination of smallpox and Ebola, immune to antibiotics.) These germs could be easier to spread and harder to treat with antibiotics. If the world is to be safe from bio terror, these threats must be faced and dealt with.

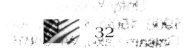

Protection

A boy receives a vaccination. The U.S. is researching various ways to protect the public from possible bio terror attacks.

Chemical Weapons

Iraqi chemical warfare bombs destroyed by United Nations inspectors after the Persian Gulf War in 1991.

More Terror Threats

THE U.S. CAN PREPARE FOR ANY NUMBER OF possible threats, but a terrorist only has to get through once to succeed. Because the U.S. is a free and open society, there are many areas where Americans are vulnerable, which is one reason the Office of Homeland Security was created—to identify and strengthen U.S. weak spots. The following issues are frequently talked about among security officials.

Chemical Weapons

Easier to make and use than bio hazards, weapons made from toxic chemicals have the potential to kill or injure large numbers of people. In 1995, a doomsday religious cult in Japan released Sarin, a deadly nerve gas, into the Tokyo subway system. Twelve people died and thousands were injured.

Despite international treaties banning their use, many countries, including the U.S., stockpile chemical weapons. The United States is trying to rid itself of its chemical weapons by 2004. Although it is unlikely that criminals or terrorists could get their hands on U.S. supplies, other countries, such as Iraq, have chemical weapons that are more easily stolen, or even sold.

Fortunately, it would be difficult for terrorists to get enough chemicals to cause mass destruction. Experts think that chemical weapons may be used by terrorists in small, easily transported quantities, just enough to terrorize the public, like in the Tokyo subway incident. Some city subway systems, such as New York and Washington, D.C., are experimenting with robotic "sniffing" devices that sound a warning if chemicals are detected.

Trucks that carry toxic loads are another worry. Security and background check procedures have been strengthened at companies that haul chemicals. Through 2001, approximately 2.5 million Americans had truck licenses that allowed them to carry hazardous materials.

Instead of transporting deadly chemicals and releasing them in public, terrorists may instead target large chemical manufacturing plants. By sabotaging these factories, terrorists could start fires that would send toxic clouds drifting over populated areas. To counter this threat, security at many of the nation's chemical factories is now being strengthened.

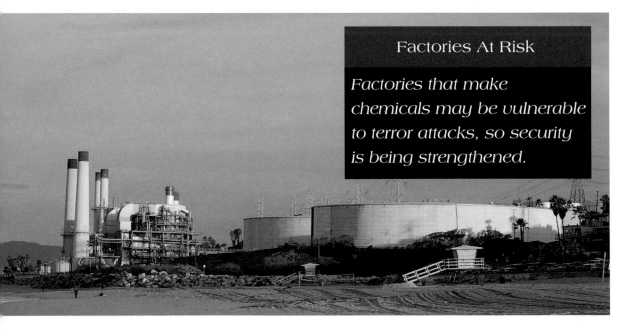

Factories At Risk

Factories that make chemicals may be vulnerable to terror attacks, so security is being strengthened.

Terror On The Subway

Firefighters wearing gas masks emerge from Tokyo's Kodemmacho subway station after the 1995 nerve gas attack by the Aum Shinrikyo cult.

Nuclear Terror

The idea of terrorists getting their hands on a nuclear weapon is a nightmare that government officials are working very hard to keep from becoming a reality. Fortunately, the chances are remote of an al-Qaeda terror cell detonating a nuclear bomb in Washington, D.C., or any other major U.S. metro area.

There are very complex engineering hurdles that must be overcome to build a nuclear bomb. However, the most difficult obstacle is obtaining the radioactive fuel, the "fissile material," that makes a nuclear bomb explode. It takes the money and resources of a major nation to manufacture weapons-grade plutonium, the kind used to make bombs.

Plutonium is a very closely guarded material, especially in the United States. In Russia, however, there are quantities of plutonium that are unaccounted for. Perhaps the discrepancies are simple accounting mistakes, but U.S. officials worry that some of the material may have been stolen or sold to terror networks.

Despite the terrifying potential for destruction, most officials believe that the technical know-how to build a workable nuclear bomb is beyond the reach of terror groups. The most likely use for stolen fissile material, they warn, is in a "dirty" bomb. These devices use regular explosives to spread the highly radioactive plutonium over several city blocks, creating terror and making the area uninhabitable for months or even years.

A nuclear power plant is another vulnerable target that may tempt terrorists. By flying a jetliner into a reaction chamber, or exploding a truck bomb nearby, radioactive contaminants would likely be released into the atmosphere, causing mass evacuations of nearby populations. To prevent such an attack, U.S. nuclear power plant security is now being reinforced. Some anti-terror experts are calling for anti-aircraft guns and a permanent military force to protect the nation's nuclear reactors.

A truck loaded with plutonium-contaminated waste travels to a permanent storage facility in New Mexico.

Welcome
CRYSTAL RIV
ENERGY COMP

Florida
Power

W. POWER LI

Heightened Alert

Armed with an M-16 rifle, a sheriff's deputy stands guard outside Florida's Crystal River Energy Complex, which includes a nuclear power plant.

Vulnerable Food Chain

Workers box chicken thighs at a North Carolina food processing plant.

Food and Water

The Office of Homeland Security and the Department of Agriculture have asked the nation's farmers, and anyone else who works in agriculture, to be on the alert for terror attacks to the U.S. food supply. The Bush administration is also asking Congress for money to add more food inspectors.

Today, only a tiny percentage of imported and domestic food is tested for contamination. Still, it would be very difficult for terrorists to poison food and cause deaths on a massive scale. Unscheduled spraying by cropdusters would raise alarms. Even if it didn't, the contaminated crops probably wouldn't be potent enough to sicken people. After working their way through the food processing chain, most crops go through a sterilization procedure, especially heating, which is designed to kill most germs. Still, many food-processing plants are boosting in-house security, watching food handlers closely, and making sure no one from the outside can easily sneak into unguarded facilities.

One sad fact about the food industry is that approximately 5,000 people in the U.S. already die each year from food poisoning. Millions of others get sick. Even if terrorists successfully poison a shipment of food, the crime might go unnoticed. Since one of their main goals is to gain attention, terrorists might not think the food chain is an attractive target.

Poisoning a city's water supply, on the other hand, might seem at first like an easy way to kill millions of people. In fact, most experts agree it would be very difficult for terrorists to kill people this way. In the U.S., drinking water is treated with chlorine, which kills most germs. Even if terrorists tried using some kind of poison or toxin in the water, they would need a huge amount.

Water Supply

A reservoir southeast of San Francisco Bay, California.

Defense analyst Jeffrey Danneels of Sandia Laboratories told *Newsweek* magazine, "Approximately four dump-truck loads of sodium cyanide mixed into a one-million-gallon reservoir are required to yield a lethal dose to users." Since most big-city water reservoirs store between three and 30 million gallons, the terrorists would need many dump-truck loads of poison in order to sicken people. Even if they could find and transport this much poison, the terrorists would obviously attract quite a bit of attention from security guards at the reservoirs.

Water purification plants would probably make easier targets for terrorists. After water is drawn from a reservoir, it is purified, then kept in holding tanks until needed by consumers. Because there is less water in the holding tanks than in reservoirs, terrorists would need less poison. To counter this threat, city water facilities are increasing security. They are also stepping up filtration and ultraviolet disinfection, which destroys the DNA of most living organisms, including anthrax spores.

A water purification plant, where water drawn from a reservoir is made safe for drinking.

Glossary

antibiotic

A substance used as a medicine to destroy or stop the growth of harmful germs in the body. Cipro is the most common antibiotic used to treat the anthrax bacteria.

combat air patrol

A patrol of fighter aircraft stationed over an area (usually a military task force) that destroys enemy aircraft threatening to attack.

Pentagon

The huge, five-sided building near Washington, D.C., where the main offices of the U.S. Department of Defense are located.

vaccine

A weakened form of a micro-organism that causes disease, which is injected into a body. The body then develops immunity to infection, even if exposed to the actual disease.

weapons of mass destruction

Weapons that kill or injure large numbers of people, or cause massive damage to buildings. When people talk about weapons of mass destruction, they are usually referring to nuclear, biological, or chemical weapons.

Where On The Web?

http://www.whitehouse.gov/homeland/

From WhiteHouse.gov, the official site of the Office of Homeland Security includes information on what the government is doing to make America more secure from terrorist attacks.

http://www.af.mil/news/noble/index.shtml

This site by the U.S. Air Force provides information, news, and photos about Operation Noble Eagle and homeland defense.

http://www.terrorism.com/index.shtml

The official site of the Terrorism Research Center is dedicated to informing the public about the phenomena of terrorism and information warfare. The site features essays and thought pieces on current issues, as well as links to other terrorist documents, research, and resources.

http://www.fema.gov/old97/terror.html

The U.S. Federal Emergency Management Agency (FEMA) gives background information on terrorism.

http://www.defenselink.mil/pubs/almanac/

Defense Almanac, a site filled with facts and statistics about the United States Department of Defense.

Index